DADDY WON'T LET MOM DRIVE THE CAR:

TRUE TALES OF PARENTING IN THE DARK

DADDY WON'T LET MOM DRIVE THE CAR: TRUE TALES OF PARENTING IN THE DARK

BY JO ELIZABETH PINTO

Daddy Won't Let Mom Drive the Car:

True Tales of Parenting in the Dark

by Jo Elizabeth Pinto

Copyright © 2019 Jo Elizabeth Pinto

Cover art created by N. Page

Brighton, CO

Published by KDP Independent Publishing Platform, July, 2019

ISBN-13: 9781080182084

DEDICATION

For Gerald and Sarah,

My incredible little family--

You were worth the wait

ENDORSEMENTS

"Blind and low vision parents face many challenges, but our kids also benefit from our resourcefulness, grit, and innovation. Jo Elizabeth Pinto discusses the challenges and opportunities with wit, wisdom, and insight. "Daddy Won't Let Mom Drive the Car" is a must-read for anyone serving diverse parent populations and for anyone who wants a fresh take on the joys and challenges of parenting.--Stacy Cervenka, Director of Public Policy, American Foundation for the Blind

"Daddy Won't Let Mom Drive the Car: True Tales of Parenting in the Dark" gives readers an honest and insightful glimpse into Jo Pinto's life as a blind mother. Pinto's ability to combine her brutal honesty and parental realism will help readers understand that parenting is messy for all of us – whether sighted or blind. Her journey of self-discovery while raising her daughter beautifully illustrates the resiliency and confidence so many blind and visually impaired parents learn to rely on while raising our families. "Daddy Won't Let Mom Drive the Car" will absolutely help to diminish many of the misconceptions of parenting without sight! Jo's work transcends beyond the blind or disabled community! It's a must-read for every parent!"--Holly Bonner, Blind Motherhood

"Pinto writes heart-warming and realistic stories about parenting as a blind person. Some stories had me laughing out loud, and others made me tear up. As a blind mother myself, I could relate to many of the stories Pinto shares, and I found myself nodding along and agreeing with some of the outrageousness that occurs when a blind parent is seen in public with her child, doing exactly what other parents are doing ... parenting. Somehow though, it is different for a blind parent. I even learned a few tips on using hot glue for art projects!

"It's obvious to the reader that Pinto loves her daughter fiercely, and I hope that one day, Sarah will read this book as a mother herself and know just how deeply her mother loves her.

"Grab a cup of coffee, grab your copy of "Daddy Won't Let Mom Drive the Car," and get ready to enjoy parenting through the eyes of a blind mom."--Lisamaria Martinez, chairwoman of the Blind Parents group for the National Federation of the Blind

TABLE OF CONTENTS

Contents

ACKNOWLEDGMENTS

First of all, this book would have been impossible to write without the one and only Sarah, who has freely offered most of the material simply by being her amazing self every day. Her dad, Gerald, has been a staunch partner in the grand adventure of her childhood journey, providing backbone when necessary, steadying my nerves now and then--and yes, driving the car.

Many of the stories in this book made their debut on Holly Bonner's Blind Motherhood blog. The piece "Enjoying Tactile Crafts with Kids" first appeared on the Web site of the National Federation of the Blind. Both the Blind Motherhood blog and the NFB Web site are excellent places to find more information about blindness in general and parenting without sight in particular.

Thank you to Stacy Cervenka of the American Foundation for the Blind; Holly Bonner, owner and chief contributor on the Blind Motherhood Blog; and Lisamaria Martinez, chairwoman of the Blind Parents group for the National Federation of the Blind— all visually impaired moms themselves--for endorsing this book. I appreciate their kind words.

I also offer sincere gratitude to my promotions assistant, Patty L. Fletcher of Tell It to the World Marketing Services, LLC, for her hard work and dedication.

I truly appreciate the members of the Brighton Writers Group for the valuable editing advice and support they have shared with me over the years. I offer special thanks to T'Nell Page for her final proofreading of this book.

Thank you to Tina Campbell for helping me cultivate my "soul garden."

N. Page created the original cover art for this book. I am very grateful.

ALSO BY THE AUTHOR

What is a family? For Rick Myers, a despondent seventeen-year-old who has just lost his parents in a car wreck, it's the four teenage buddies he's grown up with in a run-down apartment building. Fast with their fists, flip with their mouths, and loyal to a fault, the "crew" is all he has.

At least, he thinks so until he meets Daisy, an intelligent, independent, self-assured blind girl. Her guts in a world where she's often painfully vulnerable intrigue Rick, and her hopeful outlook inspires him to begin believing in himself.

But when the dark side of Daisy's past catches up with her, tragedy scatters the crew and severely tests Rick's resolve to build his promising future. Fortunately, his life is touched by a couple with a pay-it-forward attitude, forged out of their personal struggle with grief and loss. Their support makes all the difference to Rick and eventually, through him, to the ones he holds most dear as they face their own challenges. "The Bright Side of Darkness" is a story of redemption and the ultimate victory that comes from the determination of the human spirit.

This award-winning novel by J. E. Pinto is available in Kindle, audio, and paperback formats on Amazon.com.

Please look for J. E. Pinto on Facebook.

I don't remember exactly when it happened. My daughter might have been three or four years old. She may have been climbing up on the kitchen counter, quietly trying to snitch a cookie, while I was in the living room typing away on my computer. Or she may have been easing open the bottom drawer in her dad's workbench, intent on swiping his screwdrivers for the thousandth time.

In any case, I called out to her, "Sarah, I know what you're doing. The eyes in my face are broken, but the ones in the back of my head work just fine."

I was halfway goofing around when I said it. The fact that I had rock star hearing was already well-known in our house. Blind people don't necessarily hear better than those with sight, but we rely on the sounds around us, so we tend to pay attention and notice what we hear more than sighted people do.

My daughter, however, took me at my word. She rushed over to me and started examining the back of my head, combing her fingers through my long dark hair.

"What are you doing?" I asked.

"Looking for your back eyes," she said in that matter-of-fact tone kids get when they are answering grown-ups who ask dumb questions. "They must be really small. I can't find them."

"They're hard to see," I answered quickly. "They move around in my hair. They don't want to be found."

"Oh. I won't look then. They're secret." Sarah was intrigued. "Have you always had back eyes?"

"Nope." I thought fast. "I got them at the hospital when you were born. Only moms have them. Like Santa's phone number, and the magic way to know if a kid has a fever by kissing her cheek. Back eyes are just for moms."

Over the years, my daughter's understanding of my blindness has become more clear. First, she realized she had to use her words instead of pointing and whining when she asked me for M&M's® or fruit snacks at the store. Over time, she has figured out that when we play Candyland® or Snakes and Ladders®, the game goes more smoothly if she reads the dice and moves the colored tokens around the board for me. She knows I stick braille labels on canned goods in my pantry and use a text-to-speech (screen-reading) program on my computer so I can listen to e-mails and navigate the Internet. Describing our surroundings when we go out together has become almost second nature to her.

But now and then, when she has created a particularly exceptional art project or perfected a super awesome dance move, she'll still say, "Mom, Mom! Look at me! Look with your back eyes!"

Not wanting to disappoint her, I'll turn my head, face away from her, and say, "Wow! That's incredible!"

After that, I'll ask her to describe her art project or give me the details of her dance move, but she seems to need me to have that first quick look. So my imaginary "back eyes" live on, somewhere under my hair.

I keep expecting them to fade away like so many other adorable childhood fantasies have. But a few days ago, when Sarah got a fabulous new Barbie® doll for her ninth birthday, the first thing she said was, "Mom, check this out! She can move her hands and feet and everything!"

When I reached for the Barbie® doll, she put her hands on my cheeks, turned my face away, and ordered, "Look … no, look with your back eyes!"

My ten-year-old daughter won a prize this morning for completing an obstacle course at the library while making the least amount of noise. Yeah, I know. My kid. It was probably the quietest five minutes and eleven seconds she's ever had in her whole waking life, and most of her sleeping life, too.

The obstacle course had been designed to make noise. Two library staff members presided over it, one with a timer and the other with a decibel meter.

First Sarah put on a hula skirt and danced for thirty seconds. She was proud of her hula moves, having learned some basic techniques in an after-school dance program she attended last year.

Then she ditched the hula skirt and picked up three round wooden sticks, a little longer than pencils.. The challenge was to balance one stick crosswise on the other two and carry it a few yards without touching it or dropping it on the linoleum floor, which would make noise. Unlike most of the kids, who stood up and walked or scurried with the sticks, Sarah bent over and tiptoed with them close to the ground. That way when she dropped the stick she was balancing and it hit the floor, it barely made a sound.

After the sticks came a tunnel made of jingle bells, toy tambourines, maracas, and other noisy nuisances. Most of the children who ran the course before had bulled their way through the tricky tunnel, choosing to get it over with quickly and move on. But my crafty kid got down on the floor and slithered underneath the beads and bells, missing most of them altogether.

Then Sarah encountered a relay. She had to carry a spoon in each hand, one holding a plastic egg with beads in it and the other holding a cat toy. Again, she crouched down close to the floor so if she dropped her treasures, they wouldn't make noise. She didn't drop them.

Next Sarah had to roll a die to see if she was required to honk a horn. Luck was not in her favor. She squeezed a bike horn. It squawked, and she moved on. She had to sit on a balloon and bounce, but she took the shock in her knees and barely touched the balloon.

Sarah's last test was to roll in an office chair that had bells and bead shakers tied to it. She scooted slowly and carefully over to a green bucket and dropped a ball gingerly into it. The bucket had jingle bells in the bottom, but she dropped the ball in so gently it hardly disturbed the bells.

The decibel meter didn't go over fifty the entire time Sarah ran the obstacle course. The average reading on the meter while nobody was running the course was forty-one.

I asked her how she managed to do the course so silently. She said, "I watched what other kids did that made noise, and figured out some tricks."

Hmmm. Now if only I could come up with a way to keep her that quiet around the house without letting her hang out in front of a TV or a computer screen.

It came to me as we walked home from the library that Sarah has had a lifetime of experience with auditory stealth tactics, unlike the other kids she had run the obstacle course with, whose parents rely on their sight to supervise them. That prior experience may have given her an advantage on the obstacle course. Not that she's an overly sneaky child, but all children try to see what they can pull over on their parents now and then.

Since I depend on my sense of hearing to keep track of everything in my environment, Sarah has had a lot of practice with moving silently when she wants her whereabouts to be undetected. For the most part, she's given up on secrecy.

When she was a toddler, I put a plastic box of Tic-Tacs® in her pocket or taped it to the back of her shirt so I could hear it rattling and keep tabs on her by the sound. As she's gotten older, I've taught her that answering me when I call her name, especially outside our house, is absolutely non-negotiable. Otherwise, we stop whatever we're doing and go straight home or, if that's impossible, sit out the fun till it's time to leave. We've only had to walk away from the park and the swimming pool once or twice; the lesson has stuck.

Sarah and her friends are often surprised how much I can tell about what they're doing by the sounds I hear. I usually know which snacks they're grabbing from the fridge, what they're watching on TV, who's getting excluded from the latest crazy game they've concocted, and when somebody needs a hug and why.

After all, it's the job of a mom to have a handle on what's happening with her child, always and everywhere. If she doesn't have eyes to see, she better have ears to hear.

"Mommy, what's a street walker?"

The question took me by surprise. I paused at the corner a block away from the school, ready to cross the street, with my guide dog's harness in one hand and my second grader holding tightly to the other. The wind sent the dry autumn leaves scuttling around our feet.

"Well …" I thought fast. "A street walker is someone who …. someone who goes around looking for trouble. Where did you hear that word? Anlyn, forward."

My daughter Sarah trotted to keep up as we crossed the busy street. "A mean boy in my class called me a street walker because I have to walk places with you and Anlyn all the time instead of riding in a car. Everybody laughed at me. I wish you could drive like other moms."

I bit back a chuckle, but the guilt was right on its heels, followed closely by doubts and misgivings. How would having a blind mom affect a child socially? All blind parents worry about it. All blind parents dread the day their children come home with it for the first time—the teasing, the discomfort. But street walker? Seriously? Still, at least neither kid had known what the word actually meant. I mentally pushed my worries aside and dragged myself back to the moment at hand.

"Hmmm," I said aloud as we turned left toward home, "if I drove like other moms, what would we miss?"

Sarah wasn't sure at first, but before we made it to our house, we stopped to blow the seeds off some big white dandelions for good luck. We paused to sniff some pretty pink flowers growing by the sidewalk. Sarah picked up three interesting rocks, a handful of acorns, and a perfectly round pine cone for me to tuck into my jacket pocket.

"We'd miss our nature adventures," she decided.

"Exactly," I agreed. "Besides, you know your way around this half of the city better than any of your friends. They get in their parents' cars and don't pay attention to where they go. You're my little navigator, aren't you? Now, I'm going to call your teacher."

"No, don't! I'm not a tattletale!"

"Don't worry. I was a kid once, too—a long time ago. I won't ruin your reputation."

Two mornings later, I went with my daughter to school. While the kids sat on the sharing rug, my guide dog lay sedately on the floor in front of them. For fifteen minutes or so, I told the class about service dogs and how they work for blind people—helping them navigate traffic, guiding them in and out of stores and restaurants, etc, and how they're allowed to go anywhere the public can go.

"Wow, Sarah's lucky," one classmate breathed as the kids took turns petting Anlyn's soft tan coat. "Her mom gets to take her dog everywhere."

"So Sarah?" the teacher asked, in a question I had rehearsed with her, "what's it like to have a blind mom?"

"Well," my little girl said, in an unrehearsed answer, "it's like a regular mom, except Daddy won't let her drive his car."

When my sighted daughter was a toddler, I worried that as her blind mom, I'd miss out on exploring arts and crafts with her. Coloring books, paint-by-numbers, water colors—everything marketed for kids was visually oriented. At least there was playdough, that last bastion of hope. Playdough was meant to be touched, molded, squished between chubby little fingers, and occasionally even tasted. But there were so many more projects and materials that seemed inaccessible to me, geared only toward the sense of sight.

Soon I started wondering how I could combine the visual aspects of arts and crafts with the tactile. Sarah loved color from a young age. She would reach for women's bright blouses, neon hair bows, and sparkling necklaces long before she could talk. I was anything but a crafter by trade. But I decided if I could add tactile elements to Sarah's artistic sense from the beginning, she would grow up with them as a normal part of her world, not as a special approach her blind mom needed to enjoy her art projects.

As soon as Sarah started scribbling with Crayons® and paints, I began cutting out triangles, diamonds, and other shapes from tissue paper and cardboard. I helped her glue the paper shapes around the edges of her masterpieces, thus turning the flat pages into raised collages I could touch. I bought puffy, fuzzy, and sparkly stickers so she could add texture to her creations. The day she asked me to help her glue clean Popsicle® sticks onto construction paper in the shape of a house so she could color between the sticks, I felt victorious. My preschooler was catching on!

The tactile aspect of Sarah's art soon became as much her idea as it was mine. Arts and crafts turned into a visual and textural collaboration, and the gathering of the materials was often as much fun as the creation of the projects themselves. Anything we found could become part of art projects—pebbles from our garden, yarn and ribbon, dry leaves in the fall and fresh ones in the spring and summer, the acorns that dropped from the trees every autumn with their little top hats that came loose when they dried. Beads, dry beans, feathers shed by our parakeet, pine needles, stray buttons, bits of cloth, we used them all. Glitter and sequins became a focal point in Sarah's arts and crafts repertoire from the time she got old enough to keep them out of her mouth.

At first plain school glue worked for us, but eventually we needed a strong multipurpose craft glue. We probably should have used a hot glue gun for some of the heavier items. But I've lost a few battles with glue guns in my time and have chosen not to engage in further conflicts. If you insist on hot glue, devote a small electric skillet to crafting. Leave an inch or so of glue permanently in the skillet. When you need it, simply reheat the glue till it liquefies, then brush your items carefully across the surface of the glue and affix them to your project. Hot glue burns like molten lava and is not easily rinsed from skin. Don't let children touch the glue or the skillet.

As Sarah got older, we built three-dimensional figures out of miniature marshmallows, pipe cleaners, and uncooked spaghetti noodles. Over the years we've made clay pots and Christmas ornaments, painted sugar skulls, fashioned jewelry and bead art, and experimented with tie-dying, sewing, weaving, and crocheting. Some crafts Sarah took up and put down quickly; others she has stuck with for a while. Some she has started, left, and returned to.

She eventually got interested in drawing and painting without tactile elements, and I've encouraged her wholeheartedly in those endeavors.

Whether Sarah pursues arts and crafts as a hobby or simply views the work of others for pleasure, I believe her early introduction to its tactile aspects will add a new dimension to her experiences for the rest of her life. If she decides to craft or create art, the childhood memories of her tactile projects may influence the way she expresses herself as an adult. If she takes in art for pleasure, she may perceive what she views or touches on a different level than she otherwise would have.

I know this much—on our way home from school at age ten, she still stops on the sidewalk and says, "Hey, there's a perfect pine cone. It'll look awesome on the Christmas tree with glitter. And I see three little white rocks that'll be great for something. I'm putting them in your purse."

The sidewalk slid beneath my boots. A long second hung in the air, a second when I knew I was going down and there was nothing I could do about it. Then I pitched forward and sprawled on the icy concrete in front of Taco Bell®, struggling to catch my breath.

"Mom! Mommy, are you okay?" My seven-year-old tugged on my arm, and my guide dog pushed her cold, wet nose into my face.

I did a quick injury assessment as I fought off a barrage of sloppy dog kisses. Nothing warm and sticky; I wasn't bleeding. My joints all seemed to work, more or less.

I tried to smile reassuringly. "Give me a minute. I'll be fine."

"Mom, get up," my daughter Sarah urged, still tugging. "Please get up."

"I'm coming. My knee is sore, that's all. The sidewalk is slippery. I have to get up slowly so I don't fall again."

I heard someone approaching, then passing and unlocking a nearby car. I wondered briefly why the passerby didn't stop, then let that thought go. One more busy person in a world of busy people. Sarah suddenly left her position beside me.

"You could help her up, you know!" she burst out from a short distance away. I could hear the glare in her voice. "It's not nice to laugh at her!"

"Sarah!" I called, concerned. "Over here!"

By the time Sarah came back to me, I had gotten to my feet. We started walking home, carefully avoiding the treacherous patches of ice on the sidewalk.

"That man in the SUV laughed at you because you fell," Sarah said, still outraged. "I made a mean face at him."

"I appreciate the way you stick up for me, Sarah," I told her. "You have a strong sense of justice, of what's fair and what's not. But you have to be careful how you speak to people. That was a grown man you just told off. Luckily, he chose to get in his SUV and drive away. But what if he had yelled at you, or even pushed you or something?"

Sarah wasn't sure what to say about that; she just shrugged.

So far, as a little girl, she's been mostly unchallenged in her attempts at social justice. But as her mother, I worry about her safety as her image in the world changes from small and cute to tween and snarky. I've never asked her to speak up on my behalf; her support has come naturally. She's been a spitfire from the time she learned to talk, not just when it comes to her blind mother. She speaks up for bullied kids at school and mistreated stray cats and baby birds in our neighborhood.

She may become a fierce advocate for social justice as she gets older. But I don't want her to feel like she's expected to become one because her mother is blind. There's a fine line between feeling obligated to advocate and feeling inspired to do so. And until she figures this all out and learns to pick her battles—God help us as we navigate her teen years together—I'll be praying that she's protected by the best angels Heaven has to offer. She'll need them.

I got a late start as a mom. My little girl was born when I was in my mid-thirties. When I show up at her school for classroom parties and field day events, some of her friends think I'm her grandma. The fact that many of their mothers are almost young enough to be my daughter creates an interesting time warp for me.

The time warp is amplified by the fact that, as any mom will tell you, kids are living self-esteem busters. Especially little girls. They're quick to let you know about your new gray hairs or any blemishes that appear on your face, the coffee you drip on your shirt, the dress that starts to fit you a bit too tightly. If they see a lady on a TV commercial whose smile has gotten three shades brighter because she just tried a new teeth-whitening product, they'll recommend the product to you the first chance they get. My sweet angel, Sarah, is no exception. She means no harm by it; she comes by her blunt remarks as honestly as any other kid born without filters.

So while the truth of my advancing age is no surprise to me, it hit home for me in a new way the other night. My daughter got right in my face with reality--literally.

At bedtime, she read aloud to me from one of her "Scholastic News®" handouts. They're miniature newspapers passed out periodically in classrooms around the country, and the one she chose this time featured ways wild animals beat the summer heat. We read about hippos in Africa whose bodies make their own sticky sunscreen, kit foxes in Arizona whose furry paws enable them to run across the scorching sand, and silver ants in the Sahara Desert whose shiny backs reflect the heat of the midday sun.

The strangest animal we encountered was the thorny devil, a spiny lizard from the deserts of central Australia. Because it lives in such an arid environment, the thorny devil collects water by letting scarce rainfall and nighttime dew pool up in the grooves between its spines. Then the precious water trickles along the grooves on the lizard's body, eventually ending up in its open mouth.

As Sarah read, she reached out and stroked my forehead and cheek. I sighed, enjoying the unexpected caress. For a moment, I was lulled into a false sense of contentment.

Then Sarah traced the lines on my forehead and around my eyes with the tip of her index finger. "Mom, you don't have spines, but you have grooves."

"Grooves?" I frowned. "I have grooves?"

Sarah's index finger moved down to my cheek and began tracing around the curve of my nose toward the place where my lips parted. "If you sit outside when it rains, does the water collect in these grooves and trickle into your mouth?"

So much for any last hope I might have had of being a reasonably attractive woman of middle age. "What in the world are you talking about?"

"The lines on your forehead and around your eyes and lips."

After I finished tucking Sarah into bed, I asked her dad about the state of my complexion, since as a blind person, the thought of wrinkles had never really crossed my mind. I knew elderly people got wrinkles, but my face still felt as smooth under my fingertips as it ever had, and I'd never really given the idea of lines around my eyes and mouth a passing thought.

"You look fine. Not young, not old," the father of my child said in a maddeningly offhand way, hardly glancing up from his hockey game. "Nobody would believe you if you said you were thirty; nobody would believe you if you said you were fifty. Don't worry about it."

"Don't worry about it? Really?" I muttered as I walked away. "Easy for you to say! You can see yourself in the mirror!"

And there I have it. My daughter tells me I look like a thorny devil, and her dad says not to worry about it. I think I'll sit out on my front porch tomorrow. There's rain in the forecast.

My husband and I took our daughter Sarah to see the 2017 Brighton High School production of "Fiddler on the Roof" one spring Saturday evening. The cast, crew, and orchestra did a great job. Hyacinth Phonthongsy, a family friend, was the violin player.

I've probably seen the play a half a dozen times in my life, at one place or another. But watching it with my third grader gave me a new perspective on an old favorite. I worried my little girl would get bored and fidgety during the three-hour show, but her attention was glued to the stage the whole time except when she was whispering questions in my ear.

She had two main lines of questioning. One focused on arranged marriages, and the other was all about the persecution of the Jews by the Russians—or rather, why one group of people would be mean to another group just because they were different. Unfortunately, when it came to the second set of questions, I didn't have very good answers because, well, how could I put something like the Jewish pogroms in Russia, into terms that made sense to a nine-year-old when I couldn't even make sense of them myself? When I told Sarah the Russians stole Anatevka from the Jews because the Russians were fearful and selfish, she said, "How rude!" I agreed.

Sarah was more impressed with the marriages in the play, especially the first one. Not quite the stuff of Disney®, but close enough. The poor tailor got his bride, the village butcher got over it, and everybody danced.

The second marriage--a bit less Disneyesque, but okay. My

little girl has grown up in the real world. She knows about moms and dads who get married and go straight back to work, moms whose husbands are in prison, moms whose husbands aren't around at all. She could go with the flow when Hodel boarded the train and left for Siberia to be with Perchik. Sad, but life happens.

The third one threw her, hard. I thought she was going to break down in sobs when Tevye walked away from his daughter Chava after she married the Christian Fyedka. I tried to tell her in a whisper that Jewish people, and often Christians, find it very important to marry within their faiths. But she would have none of it. In her world, parents never, ever turn away from their children. Not ever, no matter what. That's how her dad and I have raised her to think. We wouldn't want her to feel any other way, right? It made sense for Tevye to walk away from his daughter in "Fiddler on the Roof"—but it didn't add up in Sarah's mind, and maybe it shouldn't have, any more than it made sense for the Russian Christians to kick the Jews out of Anatevka.

It was a somber little girl who sat beside me when the play ended. But my daughter isn't one to stay on a down beat very long. The wheels must have been spinning in her mind while the well-deserved applause for the play went on and on. After the claps and cheers finally dwindled, she said, "I'm glad I didn't live in Russia back then. I'd never let you and Daddy pick out my husband for me, just so you know."

My family and I were invited to have Easter dinner with some close friends. We had been asked to bring dessert, so I set out to make a chocolate pound cake the day before. Simple enough. I've baked zillions of cakes over the years—baking is something I do for fun. But luck wasn't with me that day, and I wasn't having fun, either.

I got the pound cake into the oven without a hitch. The trouble began when it came time to remove the sweet-smelling, dark brown cake from the round pan. I ran a spatula carefully around the edge of the pan to loosen the cake, as always, then flipped the pan over onto a glass plate—plop! Most of the cake fell clumsily out onto the plate, leaving a few jagged chunks stuck to the pan. My heart sank.

"Aw, come on!" I muttered. Then I mentally shook myself. "Oh well. It happens to the best of us. I can fix this."

I fitted the chunks carefully into the broken cake and pressed the pieces together with my fingers, still grumbling under my breath. Not perfect, but passable. The cake was warmer than I thought. I hadn't waited long enough for it to cool before I removed it from the pan.

I repaired the cake as well as I could and covered the top and sides with generous mounds of red velvet pudding. I hoped the creamy frosting had hidden my mess completely.

No such luck. When my daughter Sarah and her dad inspected the cake later, he said, "It's an ugly duckling, but I'm sure it will taste good." And she said, "You tried, Mom. That's what counts, right?"

I told Sarah she was right, but I didn't listen to my own words. In my mind, I convinced myself that I had to put a perfect cake on the table for Easter dinner. If I didn't, it would be because a blind baker couldn't make a nice-looking cake. It didn't matter that I had two college degrees and my own textbook proofreading business, that I had written and published a novel, that I was raising a beautiful little girl, or that I had contributed to and enjoyed meals with these family friends for years. Somehow, I got this Easter cake spun up in my head and decided it had to be flawless.

"Maybe you better get another dessert at the store," I suggested to my husband when Sarah was safely in bed and he was about to make an Easter Bunny run.

"No," he said, using that firm, calm voice dads get when they're talking down drama queens—of any age. "This won't be hard to fix, I promise."

He soon returned from the store with a spray can of whipped cream. I have to say, that stuff may be all chemicals, but it works wonders. When Sarah saw the cake in the morning, she breathed, "Mommy, it's perfect! Daddy fixed it!"

Perfection was short-lived, however. When we got in the car to leave for Easter dinner, I tucked the cake carefully on the middle hump between the front seats under the console. As soon as we backed out of our driveway, the cake plate slid sideways. I grabbed the edges of the plate, hoping the carefully positioned layers of red velvet pudding and whipped cream had stayed more or less intact. I started laughing as a blob of pudding sloshed messily out one side of the aluminum foil cover.

"What's so funny, Mom?" Sarah asked from her booster in the back seat.

"I guess this cake is just bound and determined to be an ugly duckling," I giggled, wondering why I had ever cared about perfection in the first place. "It broke when it came out of the pan, and it almost fell on the floor in the car."

When we arrived at the house where we were having Easter dinner, the hostess took the cake and peeled back the sticky aluminum foil. I started to apologize for the way the cake looked, but she cut me off with a good-natured laugh.

Without knowing any of my pound cake's dramatic history, she reminisced, "My mama used to say, the uglier a cake was, the better it would taste."

Her mama was right. That ugly duckling cake turned into a swan when dessert was served.

The heat wave we'd been having finally broke, so my ten-year-old daughter and I walked to Burger King® for lunch. My yellow Labrador guide dog, Anlyn, was itching for exercise, and it did us all good to get out of the house. We stopped by the grocery store on our way home to pick up a few items for dinner.

As we walked, Sarah looked at the puffy white clouds that billowed across the sky in the summer breeze. After a while, she said, "I bet Heaven is full of clouds. Some are restaurants, some are movie theaters, some are places for doing gymnastics, some are swimming pools, some are for sleeping, and some are stores where everything is free."

"That sounds nice," I agreed, wishing I could be as innocent as a child again.

I wonder how people would get between the clouds?" Sarah mused thoughtfully, half to herself.

Then she skipped with excitement, still clutching my right hand, making my guide dog stop and turn her head curiously. "Mom, Mom! I see an eagle!"

"It's probably hungry," I said. "It's looking for a bunny to eat."

"Yeah, I know ..." Sarah kept tugging my hand impatiently. "But that's how people would get between the clouds. An eagle, as big as a bus. Like that special bus that used to come get us sometimes, remember? Only the eagle would always be nice, not like those rude drivers, and people wouldn't have to pay a lot of dollar bills every time. They could just hop on its back and go to any cloud they wanted."

"That would be awesome." I smiled. "You should be in charge, kid. You have all the answers, don't you?"

"Yep," she said with unruffled confidence. "Maybe I'll be President someday, if I want to. Unless I'd rather do something else"

Excuse Me

Before my ten-year-old daughter started the fifth grade, she, one of my aunts, and I went to Target® to buy school supplies. The store was as busy as an anthill, with shopping carts squeezing past each other in the narrow aisles, employees directing traffic and helping people locate merchandise, harried adults checking items off their printed lists, and kids scurrying about looking for exactly what they needed among the seemingly endless choices on the cluttered shelves.

I waited patiently next to an end cap display, keeping a running tally in my mind as my daughter and my aunt added treasures to the growing pile in our shopping cart and checked them off our school supply list.

"Hey, I found the perfect binder," Sarah crowed with delight. "It has unicorns and mermaids and ice cream cones and sparkles and ..."

She went on waxing rhapsodic as she dropped the notebook into the cart. Fortunately, some lunchboxes on the other side of the aisle captured her attention. Otherwise, there might have been drama.

I felt a sudden bump from behind, hard enough to make me stagger. A moment later, someone grasped me by the shoulders and pushed me forward. Then unseen hands scooted my shopping cart away from me.

"Excuse me," I said, partly confused and partly annoyed.

"I need something from the end cap display," a man's voice

informed me abruptly. "You're in my way."

"You could have asked me to take a few steps forward," I answered, now much more annoyed than confused. "I didn't appreciate you touching me without permission. A simple excuse me would have done just fine."

"But you're blind."

"True enough." I nodded. "My eyes don't work, but my ears do, and so do my feet. I'm not a piece of furniture you can move around at your convenience."

"You seem really angry. I guess you're having a bad day."

I didn't dignify that comment with an answer. I'd been having a perfectly good day till I got shoved out of the way like an old suitcase. But explaining that to the person who does the shoving makes no difference most of the time. It's unacceptable for a man in our society to put his hands on a woman without a disability for any reason, except perhaps if he's saving her from imminent danger. Add a disability to the equation, though, and all bets are off. He's just trying to help, he doesn't know any better, he feels awkward and isn't sure how to start a conversation--any of these excuses are accepted as viable. If the disabled woman protests, she's considered angry, bitter, or bitchy.

The man selected the item he needed from the display and moved on. But the takeaway is, manners are universal. People with disabilities may seem difficult to approach, and speaking to us might feel awkward. That's understandable to a degree, but we're as human as anyone else. We respond to friendly greetings, pleasant conversation, or at least common politeness the same as other people do. A simple 'excuse me' goes a long way.

Sarah appeared beside me, lobbying for a brand-new lunchbox with gold sparkles on it, which I refused to buy. Her owl lunchbox from last year was still in good shape. We left the store, all set for the fifth grade. I did my best to put the exasperating incident at the end cap display behind me. It's just par for the course in the adventures of a person with a disability. Hopefully there will come a day when those of us who use mobility aids such as wheelchairs, white canes, and service dogs are seen as equal to those who travel without them. Till then, manners and friendly consideration are always appreciated.

On a recent spring afternoon, I knelt in the grass with the warm sun shining on my back and a gentle breeze cooling my face. The irises had filled the long, narrow flower bed next to my front sidewalk with fleshy new leaves, and the time had come to clear away last year's brittle, prickly tangle of dead stalks and weeds from among the thriving young plants.

I've always been blind, so gardening without looking isn't new to me. But it means I use my bare hands to distinguish flowers from weeds, healthy leaves from dead ones, and soft fresh soil from dry, hard-packed earth. Usually it's not a problem, but when I'm pulling out shriveled-up old leaves and stems without gardening gloves, which hamper my sense of touch, my hands can get pretty chewed up. And the noxious weeds called Tribulus terrestris, more commonly known as goat-heads or puncture vines, are living proof of the curse that befell Adam in the Garden of Eden. Genesis 3:18 declared, "Thorns and thistles the ground shall bring forth for you," and dag nabbit, Adam, all these centuries later I'm still yanking goat-heads out of my flower beds.

As I cleared the dead leaves away from my irises so they could soak up the nourishing spring sunshine, I got to thinking about perennials—and life. Gardening offers us some practical rules to live by.

You're bound to grab a handful of thorns now and then. It's inevitable. Get used to the prospect, and don't clutch anything too tightly till you know for sure what you're holding. That way you won't be surprised by the pokes that sting when they happen and maybe even throb for a day or two, but nothing will slice you too deeply. When you clamp down hard before you have a chance to tell what you've got in your hands, you end up with wounds that bleed profusely and are slow to heal.

Always use sharp scissors. Hacking away at something with dull blades won't do any good for you or whatever you're trying to cut through. Once you make up your mind to clip dead leaves away from your irises, or slice bad habits or toxic issues out of your life, place your scissors as close to the source of the problems as you can and make a few quick, decisive cuts. Get rid of every bit of the debris you can locate. There's no sense in leaving any of it behind. Snip it all away and make a clean start.

When you're ready to remove a weed, dig it out completely. Follow its roots down as deep as you can into the dirt with a gardening shovel, teasing them out with your fingers if you need to, even if the job takes a lot of time and effort. Otherwise, the weed will grow back before you know it and spread like crazy.

If you're lucky enough to have a child gardening beside you, don't spend all your time pushing her to get busy. She probably won't be very productive anyway. But if you listen to her as she sprinkles your new lilies and daisies with the hose, digs for worms, and fluffs up the dirt around your flowers, she'll tell you fascinating stories about the ants, caterpillars, and bees she finds. Those stories, and the observations she makes about mud and how fairies use it to build houses, and how long it takes water to fill up the drinking holes she's made for the daisies, and how lilies must be thirstier than daisies because she's had to water the lilies twice and the daisies only once, are worth much more than any grudging labor you might get from her with incessant nagging.

Don't sit too long. Get up and stretch, walk around once or twice an hour, and stay hydrated. Of course, you'll be stiff as a board for a few days even if you follow these protocols. Your legs and rear end and lower back will be sore. Sitting on the ground successfully is for kids and dogs, not grown adults. Plunk yourself down on the warm grass anyway. It's good for the soul.

Work while the sun shines. It may seem hard to believe, but a blizzard can blow down out of a clear blue sky. It happens regularly in Colorado. Early spring is enchanting, but wind and snow are never far away. The day after I tended my irises, the temperature dropped thirty degrees and a winter storm covered the flowers with a blanket of fluffy wet snow.

Which leads me to the final life lesson.

A little flexibility goes a long way. When spring plays hooky, why complain about it? Put away your gardening tools, get out your fuzzy slippers, make a cup of coffee for yourself and some hot cocoa with lots of marshmallows for your little girl, and settle down to watch a movie or play a board game together. If spring disappears, embrace winter with your whole heart. Spring will return before you know it.

I started reading a braille book to my ten-year-old daughter last night about Jackie Robinson, the African-American baseball player who broke the color barrier when he signed on with the Brooklyn Dodgers in 1947. As the book described Robinson's struggles with segregation, racism, and sometimes violence, Sarah kept repeating, "That's messed up."

The book led to a discussion of the five-paragraph essays on racism and gender inequality my daughter and her fifth grade classmates have been writing at school.

"Mom, did you know for every dollar men earn in this country, women only earn eighty cents for the same work? It was in one of the essays."

I nodded. "I know."

"That's messed up."

I had to agree.

"And did you know it used to be legal for black kids and Spanish kids to be kept out of the best schools?"

"Yes. I know."

Sarah punched a clenched fist against her mattress. "That's messed up!"

"It sure is. There are laws now that try to prevent that from happening."

"But why did it ever happen at all? It's so ... dumb and stupid."

And there we have it. Sometimes kids ask the best questions, and the hardest ones. Why did prejudice and discrimination ever happen?

I didn't have a satisfactory answer for my little girl, but the answer doesn't matter, not really. Not as much as the fact that we have a generation of children growing up in the New Millennium, many of whom truly don't understand the idea of hate at first sight. Prejudice seems to be a foreign concept to them. That may be our salvation and our best hope for tomorrow.

Because you're right, kid, the way we've been doing things so far is ... messed up.

On a warm Saturday afternoon in November, my nine-year-old daughter and I walked down the street to 7-Eleven®. Sarah had aced a spelling test the day before, and I decided to treat her to a Slurpee®.

At the convenience store counter, I started digging for loose change in my purse. The line was long, and Sarah, who thinks strangers are just friends waiting to meet her, smiled at the man in front of us.

"Well, aren't you a sweetie," the man greeted my little girl. "Are you out for a walk with your mommy today?"

"I'm getting a Slurpee®," Sarah answered proudly. "Because I got all the words right on my spelling test. Blue raspberry is the best flavor."

"I bet you help your mommy out a lot, don't you?"

I winced inwardly. The man could have focused on the spelling test or the Slurpee®, but instead he had fixated on my blindness and assumed my daughter took care of me. It happens a lot, and it doesn't get any less annoying with each occurrence.

"I guess I kind of help her," Sarah said, "when I feel like it."

That's true enough. Sarah, like any nine-year-old, can be quite helpful when it suits her. She likes to operate the steam mop on our hardwood floors. Sometimes she enjoys giving me a hand with dinner preparations or baking brownies with me. She'll pitch in with yard work because she knows her dad and I usually take her out for ice cream when it's over. But she can make a mess as well as the next kid and be just as reluctant to clean it up, too.

She's no saint because her mom is blind, nor would I want her to be.

"You know what?" the stranger in line decided. "Tell your mom to put her money away. I'm buying you that Slurpee®. I watched you two crossing the street, and you were very careful, not letting your mom walk out in front of cars or trip on the curb or anything."

Actually, I had listened for oncoming traffic and determined when it was safe to cross the street, and my guide dog had paused at the curb so I wouldn't trip. I could have made the crossing safely on my own.

I was torn. Should I let the man pay for the Slurpee®? He seemed to mean well, and Sarah is a good kid. She does a lot for me, even if her motives are less altruistic and more practical than her benefactor had likely given her credit for. As she's gotten older, she lends a hand when she sees things that need doing, simply because she sees the needs, not because she feels sorry that her mom is blind. My blindness is just a fact of her life. It's always been that way, so it isn't something she's ever questioned.

"Thank you for your kindness, sir," I broke in. "My daughter is a great kid. She did a super job on her spelling test, which is why she's getting a Slurpee®. I have the money for it, but thanks again."

"I'd really like to pay," the stranger insisted. "It did my heart good to see you two out today. A lot of kids, man, they're disrespectful. They don't care about anyone but themselves. But your little girl, she's different. Restores some of my faith in the future, you know. There oughta be more kids like her. She watches over you."

Well, if he'd quit before he added the last sentence ... But what could I do? Sarah is a polite, big-hearted girl. That much is completely true. If those qualities in her had motivated him, aside from the caretaking of her blind mom, I could understand why he wanted to treat her to the drink.

"Thank you." I still felt uncomfortable, but I smiled anyway. I wasn't ready to make a scene. There's a point where good intentions collide with misconceptions, and maybe sometimes gratitude is a better response than defensiveness—at least in front of a nine-year-old waiting for a blue raspberry Slurpee®. "Sarah, what do you say?"

Sarah thanked the man, I dropped my change back in my purse, and we made a break for the door as soon as we could.

"You know, I don't really help you that much," Sarah said when we got outside. She already had the straw in her mouth, sipping blue slush between her words.

"Maybe not in the way the man was talking about," I told her. "Sometimes you label cans and match socks with me, things like that. But mostly you're kind and polite and you try hard in school. That's how you contribute to our family right now, which is exactly perfect."

As we walked home, I thought about how blessed I've been to raise a daughter like Sarah. It's sad, though, that people like the man in line at 7-Eleven® believe young children take care of their blind parents. Who do they think changes thousands of diapers when those children are babies? Who do they think teaches those children to walk and talk, put on their socks, and eat with silverware? Do they really think it takes working eyeballs, rather than working minds and hearts, to raise families?

Holiday baking isn't as easy as it used to be.

Years ago, when I first ventured away from home, I was a confection queen at Christmastime. I arrived at holiday parties with all kinds of amazing homemade cookies and candies nobody had ever tried before, and boxed mixes never made their way into my kitchen. But these days, boxed mixes are looking really good to me. They save time, and they've started to come out in lots of unique flavors--not just boring old chocolate and vanilla cakes with a few frosting variations anymore.

My family is having a potluck Christmas party with homemade instead of store-bought gifts this year. Since I'm not a seamstress or a crafter of any kind, I've suddenly found myself back in the kitchen for real. I've baked a treat or two here and there often enough for church get-togethers and family gatherings, but this time I need a dessert for a few dozen people and several goodies to make up two festive sweet trays for the gift exchange.

In the early days of adulthood, I'd found it no trouble at all to have three or four recipes going at once--chocolate melting on the stove, the gooey part of a no-bake recipe heating in the microwave, brownies baking in the oven. But yesterday and this morning, I'm nearly losing my mind, because mixed in with all the confectionery chaos, I'm also having nine-year-old mayhem.

"Mom, wanna play Go Fish?"

"I'm busy right now. How about helping me frost this chocolate cake?"

"Okay, but see what my Fingerling® can do? I named her Bethany."

Bethany, an early Christmas gift from a family friend, is a

pink interactive monkey puppet that sits on my daughter's finger, squawking and dancing and blowing kisses.

"Awesome. Keep Bethany away from the frosting, okay? And monkeys don't eat sprinkles."

"I know. When we're done with the cake, can we go to the park?"

I try not to sigh. "Look, kid, do you think Christmas happens all by itself? I thought you were going to finish making your gift bags. This kitchen is a mess ..."

"But it's nice and sunny outside."

"And we're nice and busy inside. Now what was I doing-- oh yeah, chocolate."

I'm done at last. My family will have a luscious cake tomorrow with homemade frosting and lots of sprinkles, thanks to my daughter's decorating efforts. And two lucky people in the gift exchange will get Happy Holidays party trays with an assortment of three different treats to enjoy. But I don't know how I could have pulled it all off without boxed mixes, and I still have presents to wrap and clients who want last minute proofreading work sent out before Christmas. Being a confection queen was easier when I didn't have a child and a job at the same time.

My daughter visited the Science Museum with her fifth grade class. While on the field trip, she had the opportunity to dissect a sheep's heart. Here are the things she learned, in her own words:

1. Sheep are kind of cute, but their hearts are not. They're bloody and yucky.

2. Hearts are supposed to be all about love and romance and stuff-- forget that. The first time you see one, you'll almost pass out.

3. The left side of the heart pumps blood to a sheep's whole body. The right side only pumps blood to the lungs. So the left side works a lot harder than the right. Know what that means? Like anything that works harder, the left side is tough and strong. The right side is pretty squishy. Squishy is gross. Don't be squishy.

4. Blood clots are bad. Don't get blood clots.

My eight-year-old daughter inspired my socks off yesterday. Actually, I was wearing fur-lined snow boots, but she inspired me just the same. I went to watch her participate in her school's annual Turkey Trot with the rest of her third grade class.

Fortunately, the storm from the day before had subsided. It was still nippy out, and the ground was slippery with slightly melting snow, but the sun shone brightly.

"I won't win, Mom," Sarah had predicted glumly that morning. "I'm the slowest girl in the third grade."

"Just have fun and try your best," I had encouraged her as she left for school.

The race started, and Sarah was soon well behind the pack. She had left the winter jacket she usually wore at a friend's house. The one she had on was a hand-me-down from an older cousin. It was too big for her, and the hood wouldn't quit flopping over her eyes. She had also forgotten to put on gloves that morning. I had let her borrow mine before the race. They were too large for her hands, so she kept pushing the hood out of her face with these hopelessly floppy leather gloves that fit her like swim flippers.

I stood at the finish line as the runners came in. Soon, Sarah was left on the race course--alone. My heart sank as the seconds ticked by, lengthening into a minute, then two. A teacher went out to walk the last of the course with Sarah. I could have hugged that woman. At least my baby wouldn't have to cross the finish line all by herself, under the stares of her classmates.

Finally the dean said, "We have one more friend to cheer on."

The entire third grade began to chant in unison, "Sarah! Sarah! Sarah! Sarah!"

I held out my arms, and my little girl rushed into them, burying her face in my purple coat to hide her humiliation.

"They're all cheering for you," I told her.

"Because I came in last," she whispered.

"No!" I turned her around to face the other students. "They're cheering for you because you kept on walking. You could have given up. You could have quit, but you didn't. You kept right on walking. That means a lot."

I gave my little girl one more bear hug, then sent her off with the rest of her class to finish the school day. No more fuss. She inspired the socks off me. But at the same time, I hope she learned some valuable lessons about perseverance, about tenacity, about acting with dignity when victory doesn't come her way. Because to tell the truth, life will hand her more opportunities to practice perseverance than to take victory laps. She'll need to remember how to keep on walking when she's the only one left on the course, when the ground is slippery and her hood is falling in her eyes, when the way is long and lonely. As her blind mom, I know a thing or two about that. But blindness doesn't give me a corner on that market. Tenacity and fortitude are life skills any mom should be more than ready to pass along to her daughter when the chance arises.

Patience Muscle

My nine-year-old daughter and I visited the Adams County Fair one sweltering August afternoon. While standing in line waiting her turn to ride Penny, a brown pony with a white tail, Sarah got fidgety.

"It's taking too long," she complained as ahead of her, child after child rode the pony in a small, well-worn circle behind a flimsy metal fence. "I'm hot. I hate waiting."

I told her to exercise her patience muscle.

"My patience muscle is so stretched out it's already bleeding." Sarah let out a dramatic sigh and rubbed the bony place on her nose where it joined her forehead. "It's had enough exercise for one day."

I wanted to stroke the pony, Penny, in the same place on her soft brown forehead and ask her if her patience muscle had been exercised enough, too.

The Raspberry Bush Hotel is open for business in our front yard. When my ten-year-old daughter checked to see how the new establishment was faring on its first evening in operation, she found some flies and a couple of bees already enjoying its luxurious amenities beneath the greenery the building had been named for.

The "bug hotel" got its start at the library this afternoon. Its base is a disposable plastic plant container that a perennial originally grew in at Home Depot® or Wal-Mart®, the flimsy kind with holes in the bottom that you pop the seedling out of, dirt and all, when you transplant it in your flower garden. Sarah dropped a few rocks in the bottom of the carton to weigh it down. Then she added a fat pine cone with lots of gnarls and nooks for bugs to climb around on. She poked some cut-up drinking straws and bits of cardboard into the pine cone at odd angles to make slides and tunnels, then stuffed in bits of shredded paper so the insects would have ladders, ramps, caves, and nests to hide, sleep, and play in-- sort of a cross between a theme park and a secret getaway.

After that, my little girl added the top of the hotel, made of construction paper. Afraid bugs wouldn't be attracted to a plain old plant pot, she built an umbrella tower to keep the rain off and decorated it with bright colors. She added windows, hot tubs, and flowers--all drawn, of course, since insects would drown if the water were real. "No safety violations, Mom. We can't have any bugs getting hurt."

Then Sarah decided the bugs needed tanning beds and sun chairs. So she gathered twenty-one flat rocks and arranged them in the dirt around the hotel, under the raspberry bush, in a sort of plaza. She even colored a sign naming the establishment. I think in my next life I want to come back as a bee or an ant--only if I get to stay at the Raspberry Bush Hotel.

I don't remember where I picked up the idea. I might have read it in one of those Internet newsletters that promised to "Teach Your Child Gratitude in Ten Easy Steps." Or maybe I overheard it while shamelessly eavesdropping on other moms somewhere as they chatted about their eternally discontented children. I've picked up more than a few hot tips by sitting quietly among other parents in public places and soaking up their hard-won wisdom.

Anyway, toward the end of last summer, I started a new bedtime tradition with my daughter called Thankful Thursdays. Every Thursday night after I read to her and we pray, each of us names three or four things we are thankful for about our day. Now and then if the day has been really rough, we look back over the week for ideas. But we usually have no trouble finding plenty of gratitude material on any ordinary Thursday.

When I started Thankful Thursdays, it was all about teaching my ten-year-old to be grateful. I wanted Sarah to understand how wonderful the world truly is and how lucky she is to have a place in it. But it didn't take me long to begin learning lessons from my little girl.

The lesson that struck me first was the way Sarah turned out to be sincerely thankful for everyday blessings I might have missed if she hadn't pointed them out. Pizza. Crickets. Sleepovers. Ponytail holders that don't fit too tight and hurt your head. New Barbie® dolls and old teddy bears, the first frost of autumn, and lost library books finally found.

Then I noticed that mixed in with the thanks for chocolate milk and chicken nuggets for lunch at school, for best friends and bunnies in the bushes and gold stars on spelling tests, gratitude thoughts with more depth began to surface.

"I'm thankful I have a warm house, because that man we saw at Burger King® today didn't have anywhere to live."

"I'm happy I have lots of shoes, since there's this boy I know at school who only has one pair, and you can see his socks peeking out."

"I'm glad we don't live in the time of Laura Ingalls because I would have hated the food they ate back then, and all the hard work they had to do."

I bit my lip to keep from laughing about that one. Sarah had a point about the hard work. But she also had more of a handle on gratitude and empathy than I'd given her credit for, although she hadn't expressed those feelings aloud as often as I'd thought she should. We've been starting to build on those feelings with actions such as gathering outgrown clothes and small toys to give to people who need extra help for the holidays.

One simple step, the decision to practice gratitude, can spark a lot of contentment and positive action in life. It has for my daughter and me. Think about giving Thankful Thursdays a try. If the bedtime format doesn't work for you, gratitude can make for uplifting dinner table conversation or inspiring reflection during a long car ride. It can turn a harried lunch break into a mental refueling session. Sarah and I have even been known to race the cashier a time or two by trying to think of as many reasons to be grateful as possible before our turn comes up in the grocery store line. Thankfulness can be downright fun with some creative tweaking--and the best part is, it doesn't have to be reserved for Thursdays.

I struck gold last Saturday.

Paper gold.

My ten-year-old daughter was away, visiting relatives in another city. So I did what any mom with the opportunity would do; I cleaned her room while she wasn't there to get in my way. I tossed out broken toys, spent coloring books, and last year's Valentines. I donated old clothes and outgrown Halloween costumes that wouldn't be missed but that would have been cried over if they'd been seen as they were sent out the door. With a pang, I gave away a garbage bag full of books that my little girl had outgrown. We had enjoyed many of those books together as she learned to read, but the time had come to move on.

As luck would have it, my hometown bookstore held a parking lot sale that very day. I picked up forty books for young readers for a quarter apiece to replenish the ones I emptied from Sarah's shelves. I didn't even care what I took from the sale; I just filled a box. But as I went through the titles more carefully later, I almost cried. What a privilege to fill those empty bookshelves.

"Black Beauty." Nancy Drew. Books about basketball and gross body facts and the weather. A bit of sci fi, a few adventure tales, some history. "The Blacck Stallion." A ghost story or two. The Hardy Boys. A lot of books and authors were new to me. Sarah will probably pick and choose, find some she loves and others she doesn't like very much, and her choices may be quite different than mine were as a child. That's fine; at a quarter each, I don't care if she passes a few books along to her friends, loses one or two, trades a couple of titles for ones she likes better. She's rolling in treasure more valuable than money can buy. I feel honored that I could put it at her fingertips.

My nine-year-old daughter burst through the front door and shoved her soft-sided lunchbox into my lap full force, right on top of the braille book I was proofreading. "Mom! Bugs flew out at me! I opened the zipper, and a cloud of bugs just poofed out at me!"

"What? Wait, what?" I set aside my work, took the lunchbox, and like any respectable mom, shifted immediately into sleuth mode. "Start from the beginning. Bugs flew out of your lunchbox? What did the bugs look like? What did you do?"

"Tiny black bugs. They were disgusting. I screamed—eeeww! Then my friend Lily saw them and she screamed, and this boy Darien saw them and he screamed, too. The lunch lady ran over, and she thought the bugs were gross. so she got the custodian to clean out my lunchbox. And I didn't want to eat the food, so I got another lunch."

I kept calm on the outside, but I felt a familiar terror gripping my heart, mercilessly, like a cruel, crushing hand. The hand let go of my heart as my thoughts whirled; then it slid upward to my throat, digging viciously into my windpipe, cutting off my breath.

Who else had seen those bugs fly out of my daughter's lunchbox? Surely everybody had noticed, especially since Sarah had been such a drama queen about it. What if the custodian or the cafeteria supervisor decided Sarah's blind mom couldn't keep a clean kitchen, since she sent her little girl to school with bugs in her lunchbox? I was almost sure the bugs were harmless. They were probably just common house gnats, but still. EEEWW!

"I'm sorry about the bugs." I forced myself to speak calmly, although I was fighting like mad to keep from hyperventilating. "That must have been embarrassing. But gnats are harmless. They're just annoying little critters that eat fruit. They probably stowed away on the pineapple or the bananas we bought last night. I'll make sure your lunchbox is nice and clean for tomorrow."

I washed the lunchbox out with antibacterial soap, and when Sarah's dad came home from work that night, he flushed the kitchen and bathroom drains out with vinegar and hot water, just in case.

"Drink up, boys," he said cheerfully. "That should take care of the gnats for a while."

But it would take a lot more than vinegar and water to wash my fears away. Blind parents are three to four times more likely to be referred to Child Protective Services (CPS) than their sighted peers are. I couldn't keep from wondering if the gnats in Sarah's lunchbox would be the next issue that prompted some well-meaning school official to pick up the phone.

The first time I had to face down CPS, someone had called me in because I had a "big black mean-looking dog"—and you never know, a dog might harm a crawling baby if her mom couldn't keep watch on the situation every moment. Ballad, my second guide dog, would never have hurt a fly. Sarah used to sit on her head now and then, and Ballad would hardly wake up from her nap to shrug off the annoyance. The case was closed, unfounded.

The second time a social worker and a police officer appeared on my porch, I had brought home some groceries on a sweltering summer day. I was trying to unlock my front door, juggling a guide dog, a cranky toddler, a heavy backpack, a sack of canned goods, and a gallon of milk. Something had to go. What went was the gallon of milk, which was the reason I had gone to the store in the first place. Splat! All over the front porch. I cursed. My daughter cried. The dog began lapping up the milk, which ran like a river over my shoes and down the porch steps. I dropped the bag of canned goods in the puddle. It was my turn to cry as I squelched into the house. An hour later, I had a police officer and a social worker on my still milky doorstep, informing me that an anonymous caller said "the blind lady wasn't coping well." I told them I would have coped a whole lot better if the anonymous caller had come to my aid, mop and bucket in hand, maybe with a listening ear besides, instead of calling the social workers and the police. The case was closed, unfounded.

Next, a nosy neighbor had threatened to call CPS because I regularly took my little girl to the swimming pool by myself at the condo complex where we lived.

"Some of the other moms and I, we've been talking," she told me. "We think it's dangerous for you and Sarah to be at the pool alone."

Instead of asking her why she and the other moms didn't come hang out with us at the pool—which, in hindsight, might have been a really good question—I assured her that my daughter had worn flotation devices since infancy, that I'd been a competitive swimmer in high school and was competent in the water, that I stayed right next to Sarah as she swam and kept in verbal and physical touch with her at all times, and that I wasn't about to let the fears of the neighborhood moms limit my little girl by keeping her home from the pool I helped pay for with my HOA dues. I believed that learning to swim, at least enough to save herself from drowning, was not only a great opportunity for my daughter but also an important precaution I needed to take for her safety. So if the neighborhood moms felt the need to call CPS, they could do what they had to do and I'd take on that battle when it landed in my lap. I never heard another word about it.

Nevertheless, as a blind mom, the nagging worry about CPS lurks constantly in the back of my mind. When my daughter gets a new teacher at school or joins a different Sunday school class at church, I feel happy for the opportunity. Then she inevitably does something goofy—and perfectly normal—like wear a raggedy old jacket that's two sizes too small. You know, the kind of jacket you thought you threw in the box of cleaning rags under the kitchen sink. And the worry in the back of my mind flares up into a hot flame of fear. What if the new teacher thinks I can't dress my daughter properly? What if she decides to make the dreaded phone call? Fortunately, the teacher laughs off the incident when I explain that my kid has a very unconventional fashion sense and that she's a hoarder in training. and the flame of fear dies down to a nagging worry once again—till next time.

Thankfully, the gnats disappeared easily from my kitchen, and nobody from the school made a big deal about them. But raising kids in a fishbowl is a sad reality for disabled moms in our society. We have set incredibly narrow standards of what motherhood should look like. When people see moms who deviate from those standards, suspicion and judgment tend to be their first reactions. Most people soften their views with familiarity and education, but blind moms and those with other disabilities unfortunately get used to parenting under pressure as their children grow up and navigate the normal scrapes and scuffles of life. The good news is, I've found that most of the issues my daughter and I face are no different than the ones sighted parents and their children deal with every day. I know I'm a good mom, so in spite of the nagging worry about CPS that lingers in my mind and flares up into full-blown fear now and then, I have the confidence as a parent to face down any obstacles that come my way. Be they gnats or nosy neighbors or unknown trials of the future, I'll prevail against them one by one.

Two days before Christmas, we got a sudden snowstorm in Colorado. The storm was brief, but it left behind enough snow to cover the sidewalks with a few inches of white fluff. When the sun reappeared, my nine-year-old daughter took the initiative and bundled herself up in a long-sleeved shirt and a fleece-lined sweatshirt, a pair of jeans and some waterproof snowpants, three pairs of socks, high boots, a winter coat, mittens, and a neon pink knitted stocking cap with a pom-pom on top. Nearly as round as she was tall, Sarah hustled out the door, ready to earn a few dollars shoveling sidewalks for the neighbors on our block.

"I'll give you five bucks to do our front walk between the house and the street," I offered, afraid she might not find other takers. "You need to clear the walk along the street, and the brick path that goes to where I take the dog out. Never mind the driveway—your dad's car will pack that snow right down when he comes home."

It turned out two other neighbors let my daughter shovel for them as well.

"Your girl's a fine young entrepreneur," Dick, the kind old man from across the street, told me. "You bet I'll support that."

When Sarah had been gone for well over an hour, I started to get concerned. I had just reached for my coat, intending to venture out and search for her, when she burst through the door on a gust of frigid air. She had a small plastic bag in her hand. I figured she had gone to 7-Eleven® at the end of the street, eager to spend her hard-won earnings on candy.

She threw off her wet wrappings and marched straight to her art shelf. For the rest of the afternoon, she busied herself with glue, scissors, and who knew what, all the while gleefully hinting that I was going to love the present I would find under the tree on Christmas morning.

"It cost me ten bucks," she finally blurted out, unaware of the social taboo that generally stops people from telling others how much has been spent on their Christmas gifts.

When Sarah had half sweet-talked and half strong-armed us out of bed on the big day, her dad and I put on our bathrobes, made coffee, and settled ourselves by the Christmas tree. Before Sarah opened a single gift of her own, she dropped a small tissue paper package into my lap. I peeled off a mile and a half of Scotch Tape® and unwrapped a fidget spinner. The thumb grip was covered with yellow sequins that had been glued firmly in place.

"There's a picture of Aqua-Man® under the sequins," Sarah said. "He was all they had at 7-Eleven®, and you had to have a fidget spinner because you always spin mine while you think of what to write about on your computer. So I had to buy Aqua-Man® with my shoveling money and find a way to cover him up since he's a boy and you're a girl. Girls don't do boy superheroes, you know. I tried yellow paper, but then it wouldn't spin, so sparkles were the only way. I picked yellow because you like the sun so much. If you could see, I think you'd like the color of sunshine."

I hugged and kissed my little girl, who I decided right then must have the biggest heart in the state of Colorado.

"Mom, Mom--look!" My ten-year-old daughter stopped the shopping cart yet again and reached for another item that had caught her eye. "Brookies. They're sooo good. We have to buy these."

"We're not here to take home the store." I felt like a broken record. "I can only carry so much in the backpack, and having a credit card doesn't mean free money. I still have to pay the bank for what we buy."

"But brookies!" Sarah persisted. "They're awesome. Do you even know what a brookie is?"

"It's a fish," I said. "A brook trout. Tastes good cooked in butter."

"It is not. The bottom layer is a brownie, and the top layer is a cookie," my little girl coaxed. "How can you resist that? Doesn't it sound like the best thing ever? I ate some at my sleepover last weekend ... they're almost better than hugs and kisses."

"Those are full of chemicals and junk you don't need." I took the box of treats and put it back on the store shelf. "But if a brookie is a cross between a brownie and a cookie, I bet we can make them at home."

"How can we?" Sarah asked, half sullen and half incredulous, and still fully wanting the box I had put back. "You didn't even know what a brookie was till I told you about them, and now you think you can make them?"

"I know I can. I'm Supermom," I assured her dramatically. "To the baking aisle!"

Sarah helped me find cocoa powder, vanilla extract, brown sugar, and chocolate chips in the baking aisle. I spent more money than I would have on the boxed treats and had a heavier load to carry home, but I'd have leftover baking products to use in other recipes later. Besides, my homemade brookies would be free of artificial colors, preservatives, and other ingredients I couldn't pronounce.

Once home, I went online and searched till I found a seasonal recipe for pumpkin brookies that suited my needs. What did we ever do before Google®? The treats turned out moist and delicious, and pumpkin puree has some health benefits--although with the amount of sugar in each serving, these are definitely dessert items.

Sarah helped me with egg-cracking, stirring and mixing, and the best part--licking the beaters. The basic gist of making brookies is putting together a batch of brownies, baking them partway, then mixing up some cookie batter--this time I did pumpkin spice--and spreading that on the mostly baked brownies. Then you slide the whole pan back in the oven and bake everything till the brownies are done and the cookie layer is set. Both layers meld themselves together into one moist, delicious flavor fusion. Yum!

So, Sarah and I are both right. Brookies are the best. I've been converted. But I'm not sure anything out of a box on a grocery store shelf would have won me over. The best treats often still come out of moms' good old-fashioned ovens--even if those Supermoms do find their recipes on Google®!

Pumpkin Spice Brookies

Brownie Layer

1/2 cup (1 stick) butter or margarine, melted

1/2 cup unsweetened cocoa powder

1 cup granulated sugar

2 eggs

2 teaspoons vanilla extract

1/2 teaspoon salt

1/2 cup flour

1 cup semisweet chocolate chips

Pumpkin Spice Layer

1/2 cup (1 stick) butter or margarine, melted

1/4 cup firmly packed brown sugar

1/2 cup granulated sugar

3/4 cup pumpkin puree (not pumpkin pie filling)

2 teaspoons vanilla extract

1-1/2 cups flour

1/4 teaspoon baking powder

1/4 teaspoon baking soda

2 teaspoons cinnamon

1/4 teaspoon ground cloves

1/4 teaspoon nutmeg

1/4 teaspoon ground ginger

1/4 teaspoon salt

1 cup chopped walnuts or pecans

Instructions

1. Preheat the oven to 350 degrees. Line an 8-inch square pan with foil. Lightly grease the foil.

2. In a medium-sized bowl, mix the cocoa powder into the melted butter or margarine till the cocoa dissolves. Add the sugar and stir again. When the sugar is incorporated, add the vanilla and eggs. Add the flour; stir till the mixture is just combined. Stir in the chocolate chips.

3. Bake the brownie layer for 20 minutes, or till it's mostly set.

4. While the brownie layer is baking, combine the remaining melted butter or margarine with the two sugars, stirring till smooth. Add the pumpkin puree and vanilla. Stir to combine well.

5. Combine the dry ingredients in a small bowl. Add them to the pumpkin mixture and stir till everything is just incorporated. Fold in the nuts.

6. When the brownie layer has baked for twenty minutes, carefully spread the pumpkin batter over the top. Return the pan to the oven for another ten to fifteen minutes, or till the pumpkin layer is set. Test with a toothpick inserted into the center of the pan.

7. Cool the brookies completely in the pan before lifting out the foil and cutting the treats into squares. Store them in an airtight container.

Teachers have taken a lot of heat in the news lately. In some states, they've gone on strike for better wages and updated textbooks. In others, they've spoken out against guns in schools. After reflecting on the lively tales my daughter Sarah told me about the third grade class trip she took to Barr Lake State Park last spring, I feel sincerely inspired to give a shout out to all of you brave, awesome teachers of the world. You're amazing! When politicians rag on you for daring to want a few of the finer things in life, when parents gripe at you because you're too hard on their little darlings or don't challenge them enough or give them too much homework or don't shower them with every moment of your undivided attention, or whatever their latest beef is, smile to yourselves and let their snark roll off--like water off a duck's back, my dad would always say.

My little girl saw fish, frogs, ducks, red-winged blackbirds, and geese at the state park. A boy in her class threatened to push her into the lake and feed her to the piranhas and alligators.

"There are no piranhas and alligators in Colorado, goofball," she said. "It's too cold here."

"Then I'll feed you to the angry geese!" the boy blustered.

"Geese can be very grumpy," she told me seriously.

Sarah touched a live bullsnake--scaly and cool, not slimy--and saw a shaggy, full-sized mounted buffalo "that was even bigger than Dad."

Anyway, back to why teachers are absolutely amazing. One of the park rangers did a presentation about birds, especially chickadees, and how they puff up their feathers so they appear much larger than usual when a perceived enemy enters their territory. Then they give out their distinctive call, "Chicka-dee-

dee-dee-dee-dee-dee!" in an attempt to drive the intruder away.

A couple of the boys decided they liked the sound of the chickadee call and started to imitate it. The fad caught on, and a few more kids joined in, then more and more and more kids. This kept up till by lunchtime, four classes of third graders were chanting, "Chick-a-dee-dee-dee-dee-dee!" almost nonstop. All through lunch and back to school on the bus, the chant went on relentlessly. Sarah said, "The noise made my brain hurt."

"Chicka-dee-dee-dee-dee-dee!"

Finally, a student teacher had reached her limit. She sucked in a deep breath and yelled at the top of her lungs, "ENOUGH!"

"Her face was bright red," Sarah reported, obviously impressed. Then she asked timidly, "Mom, are teachers allowed to yell at us like that?"

"Well--" I hesitated, trying to decide what to say. Then--I couldn't help myself; I burst out laughing. "I don't blame her. I'm not sure it was the best choice she could have made, but if I were trapped on a bus with a hundred eight- and nine-year-olds babbling like chickadees out of tune, I might have yelled for mercy, too."

So here's to you--student teachers brimming with enthusiasm and still filling your bank accounts with grace and patients; teachers in the trenches who do their best to guide, motivate, and nurture our children throughout the weeks and months and years of their long school careers so they can reach their full potential as adults; and retired teachers who have finished pushing their share of chickadees out of the nest and are ready to watch them fly and hear them sing.

I can't believe how quickly the year is whizzing by. Valentine's Day is almost upon us. If you're lucky, the thought of the holiday sends visions of roses and jewelry dancing in your head. But if you're like many blind moms, Valentine's Day also gives you the jitters, because along with the romantic pampering comes yet another classroom party your kid is over the moon about. You want to attend and support your child, but hanging out with twenty-five screaming sugar-crazed maniacs in a classroom half the size of a box of chocolates, feeling like your eardrums are on the edge of disintegration, isn't your idea of a good time.

Don't worry. As a blind mom and a Valentine's Day veteran, I've come up with a few survival tips. Most of them will work for other parties—Halloween or harvest festivals, Thanksgiving dinners, Christmas or winter break parties----but Valentine's Day bashes offer some extra challenges.

The first challenge is that your child will usually be asked to sign and pass out Valentine cards for his or her classmates. A printed list of names should be sent home well in advance of the party. By this point in the school year, you should hopefully be e-mailing regularly with your child's classroom teacher. Ask for an electronic copy of the class list so you can enlarge the print or braille it, then help your child spell the names correctly. A very young child may simply sign premade cards with his or her own name. An older kid can make cards and write the names of the other students, perhaps while you dictate them aloud letter by letter.

The next challenge is that your child will often be asked to decorate a box, bag, or other container for receiving Valentines. An empty plastic ice cream tub with a handle makes a good base. Help your kid measure and cut a piece of construction paper so it will wrap snugly around the tub. Then lay the construction paper flat and let your little artist decorate it with stickers, yarn, buttons, glitter, ribbons and bows left from Christmas wrapping, or anything else that adds color and texture. Crayons®, markers, and colored pencils also come in handy. When the masterpiece is finished, wrap the construction paper snugly around the ice cream container, taping it down in several places underneath where the tape can't be seen. Be sure to tape the last edge well so the paper stays in place. It's also a good idea to tape the paper edges along the bottom of the tub and at the rim in several places, using clear tape so it won't be noticed.

Contact the teacher ahead of time to find out what you can bring to the party or how you can volunteer, if you're interested. Some teachers will be more receptive than others to your help as a mom with a visual impairment. If you want to volunteer but are turned down, pushing the issue head-on amidst the plans for a class party isn't the best time. Teachers need classroom help all year long. Save your activism for a less stressful moment. Offer to bring napkins or doughnuts to the party. I usually try to contribute something I can carry easily in one hand, leaving my other arm free for a guide dog or a cane. Then, while at the party, engage with the kids. Help one with an art project, let another read to you, join in a game, ask about the cookies a group at a table is decorating. Let the teacher see you interacting with the class; he or she may decide you can help out in spite of your blindness.

If you have a friend whose child is in the same class as yours, consider meeting up at the party. Someone who can describe the lay of the land and let you know what games the kids are playing and what funny things might be happening is invaluable. Facing the mayhem with an ally is definitely a plus. However, having your own escape plan in case you need to leave the party is also helpful. It's awkward if you need to leave but you've depended on someone else for transportation, and you have to stay till that person is ready to depart.

Be self-contained at the party. Bring your own beverage in case there isn't anyone available to assist you in getting one. Twenty-five children rushing around in a small classroom, desks and chairs in disarray, a scattering of parents, and off-the-charts noise level, can overwhelm even the bravest guide dog or the most well-oriented person. I like to carry a snack in my purse so I don't look conspicuous by not eating, even though my daughter is very good about sharing her treats.

Speaking of sharing treats, be careful not to depend on your child too much. Greet his or her friends, make small talk with the other parents and the teacher if they allow it, and let your kid guide you on how open to be about your blindness. During the early grades, my daughter asked me to braille names on the Valentines for her classmates. She wanted everyone to pet my guide dog. Now, as a third grader, she's becoming more reserved about having a mom with a disability. I've taken my cues from her and backed off some, foregoing the braille Valentines and making sure my guide dog stays unobtrusively by my chair where she belongs. It's normal for kids to go through stages of openness and reticence about their parents' disabilities at different ages, so don't take it personally.

The most important party tip of all is, try to have fun. Your kid knows when you're faking it. It's easy as a blind mom to believe you're the only one who's overwhelmed and doesn't know what to do with herself, but it simply isn't true. A few of the parents are party naturals. They fix the food trays perfectly. They set up all of the crafts just right. But most of the moms and dads feel a bit like clumsy giants among those tiny desks and chairs, just as you do. So take a deep breath and relax. With love in the air and these party tips, hopefully the upcoming Valentine's Day celebration at your school will go off without a hitch.

I'm on my third day with a raging migraine. So my nine-year-old daughter appointed herself as my house nurse this morning.

A "house nurse," Sarah explained, brought food and water, fluffed pillows, and kept her patient comfortable. She gave me a plastic pencil box with beads in it to shake when I wanted to summon her--the closest thing she could find to a bell. She called herself a "house nurse" as opposed to a "real nurse" because she told me straight up she "wouldn't do blood or anything else disgusting."

I thought it was smart of Sarah to limit her duties to what she felt capable of handling--no blood, no body fluids. Fair enough. My little girl knows her own mind and isn't afraid to set her boundaries. There are adults who could learn from her, including her own mom at times.

Soon after her dad left for work, my house nurse brought me breakfast in bed. The meal consisted of a half a dozen pineapple chunks on a plastic Disney Princess® plate, a cup of pink raspberry lemonade with a few more pineapple chunks in the bottom to make it tropical, a chocolate Laffy Taffy®, and two orange Starburst® candies from her Halloween haul. How could I ask for more? When I knew Sarah wasn't watching, I slipped the candy back into her smiling jack-o'-lantern bucket and sneaked a Nutrigrain® bar from the kitchen cupboard.

At lunchtime, my house nurse insisted her patient needed fresh air. In spite of my protests, she half coaxed and half coerced me into putting on my heaviest bathrobe and sitting out on the front porch with her. The breeze was cool, but the sun was sort of warm, and the crisp fall air did feel a little nice. Lunch consisted of a very well-toasted raisin bagel with lots of melted butter, a handful of Saltine® crackers, a fun-sized caramel Twix® bar, a little piece of a glazed doughnut, and a leftover brownie from Thanksgiving.

I still have the migraine. Most times, there's nothing to do but wait for those to burn themselves out. But I swear, I've got the best house nurse on the planet.

After a big shopping trip to stock the pantry, my daughter and I sat on the kitchen floor one Saturday afternoon marking canned goods in braille. I felt overwhelmed by the dozens of cans that needed to be labeled and put away, which led to a few sharp jabs from my conscience. My little girl was stuck doing a boring job while her friends were probably outside playing because her blind mom couldn't see the labels on the canned goods in her own kitchen.

Sarah soon put an end to my internal guilt trip. As I punched out sticky tapes with my braille label maker, she made a long line of cans across the floor.

"Next," she said in her best nurse's voice. "Hello, Tomato Soup. The doctor will see you now. Wow, you've got a dent! What happened?"

"Food fight," Tomato Soup answered in a gruff, deep tone.

Sarah took the label from me, peeled off the adhesive back, pressed it on the can, and scolded, "Really, a food fight? You need a Band-Aid. There it goes, right across that dent. Behave yourself, okay?"

She put the can on the counter and called briskly, "Next. Chili Beans … how are you today? No salt added … you need to work on your diet, don't you?"

I started making the label.

"Next. Baked Sweet Potatoes … are you half baked or all done?"

And so it went. We giggled and worked and had such a good time, the job was finished before we knew it. All it took to turn a chore into a fun game was a child's vivid imagination and a generous helping of laughter.

Labeling those cans for my pantry has become one of my most treasured memories from Sarah's school age years. I learned two important lessons from the time we spent together. The first is, no guilt. Families have different needs, and children pitch in where their talents fit. If that means my kid reads labels so I can mark cans after we go shopping, so be it. And if she can make the job fun and interesting, so much the better.

The second and most important lesson I learned is, blind or sighted, enjoy the spontaneous moments with your child as they come along. You can't plan them, you can't create them, and you can't predict when they will happen. But you can soak them up and squeeze every drop of joy out of them when you find yourself in the midst of them, and treasure the memory of them afterward.

My daughter and I took my guide dog, Anlyn, to a blessing ceremony on the lawn outside St. Augustine's Catholic Church this afternoon. The ceremony was held in honor of St. Francis of Assisi, the patron saint of animals. Maybe it was no wonder Sarah said she saw 240 migrating butterflies and eleven ladybugs while we were out today. She said we'd have good luck all year long.

Gathered on the lawn were families with their pets--mostly pooches--everything from standard poodles to teacup chihuahuas, from tiny new puppies to noble search and rescue dogs in their service vests. Sarah fell in love with a pair of "basket hounds"--you know, the kind with the big ears that drag on the ground. She saw a couple of "very twitchy" cats, some baby guinea pigs in a see-through plastic crate, a half a dozen parakeets huddled in a travel cage, and one pet duck doing its level best to disappear in the newly mown grass. She told me it was a good thing the ceremony was short or she might have died of cuteness overload.

The ceremony was quick and simple, either because the clouds had gathered to deliver more fake rain--ten drops and a spit, as usual--or because the priest wasn't a Noah type. Animal blessings I'd been to in the past had involved standing in line for a personal prayer, a sprinkle of Holy Water or an anointing with oil, and a St. Francis medal for my dogs' collars. But this time, the priest simply prayed, thanked God for our stewardship of animals and the unconditional love our pets give to us, then dipped a long palm branch in Holy Water and sprinkled the zoo en masse. The entire blessing took about ten minutes, and as we left for home, a smattering of raindrops fell. I guess the Good Lord decided to add His agreement to what the priest had done.

"Anlyn didn't like the water much," my little girl observed. "Neither did the cats. I think the duck loved it, though. It stretched its wings and neck way out."

While chatting with a blind friend recently, I finally understood an aspect of myself I probably should have figured out more than thirty years ago, when I was still in my teens. The revelation hit me like a fist between the eyes.

I've never been a particularly spontaneous person, to say the least. If we're going to be honest, I've driven my friends and family out of their collective minds over the years because of my often maddening attention to detail. In my defense, that attention to detail has also saved some of their collective butts at times, but those stories are best left for long evenings of tipsy reminiscing or moments when mild blackmail becomes necessary.

The point that struck me during my recent conversation is that spontaneity is a valued personality trait in the general population. But for people with disabilities, especially those of us not blessed with easy transportation options, it's a luxury, a privilege, an outlook that's risky and often just plain too exhausting to cultivate.

As a teenager, I used to giggle about women who hauled around handbags that resembled suitcases. You know, the kind that made them totter precariously to one side as they walked, the kind that doubled as deadly weapons when swung at muggers or stray dogs in a pinch. Now I carry what I call my "Mary Poppins® purse." I've learned as a blind traveler that, especially with a child tagging along, I may not always be able to get what I need on the go. So I tend to bring everything that might come in handy for the day when I leave the house. Need a lamp, a measuring tape, or a hat stand? I just might pull one out of my oversized purse when it's called for.

I'm a hopeless planner. When I returned to college in my early thirties, working part-time and taking a full course load, I sat down at the beginning of every semester with all of my class schedules. Breaking each syllabus down week by week, I figured out in meticulous detail which reading and writing assignments I needed to complete every weekend so I wouldn't fall behind at any point. Later when my daughter started elementary school, I did my best to keep her on a similar schedule. She lacked my regimented personality and resisted my organizational efforts with every ounce of her free-wheeling spirit.

I'm a stickler when it comes to putting dishes and groceries in the same places on my kitchen shelves. Otherwise, my family might end up eating spaghetti flavored with applesauce--yes, it happened once. Nobody died.

I try very hard not to forget things at the grocery store during shopping trips because it's difficult for me to know when I'll make it back to purchase the missing items. At the end of a stressful day recently, after dropping well over two hundred dollars at Target® and arriving home to find we had forgotten toothpaste, I didn't know whether to curse or cry.

"It's just toothpaste," my husband Gerald said. "I'll get some over the weekend."

"I know." I sighed. "But I hate loose ends."

"God ... it's just toothpaste," he repeated. "Stop kibbitzing."

That's the thing. I'm on guard, a lot. There's always something to keep tabs on. Have I gotten all of my printed items read to me while a sighted person is on hand, since I don't know when the next reader will come around? Do I have all of my errands planned on the same day when somebody will be able to drive for me? Have I remembered everything on my shopping list so I won't have to return to the store?

Now who said I was supposed to be spontaneous? Oh, right--I'll try to fit that in. Maybe I'll have time ... at two-thirty next

Tuesday afternoon.

The spring my daughter turned nine years old, each student in her class received a young cabbage plant through the Bonnie Plants 3rd Grade Cabbage Program, which seeks to inspire a love of gardening in children across the country. Sarah and her dad planted her cabbage on the sunny south side of our house, next to her cherished raspberry and blackberry bushes.

What an adventure! My little girl sheltered that cabbage under a bucket during a late spring snowstorm. Her dad helped her build a chicken wire cage around the plant to keep the leaves from becoming food for raiding rabbits, and the cabbage outgrew its cage three times. We carried gallons of water to the plant on hot days and fertilized the soil around its roots with old coffee grounds as it grew. We sprinkled the leaves with pesticide powder when the bugs started to eat holes in them. Nurturing a cabbage plant is a lot of work.

Finally, after three and a half months, the cabbage began to split. That meant it had finished growing, according to my dad, who had worked in the fields as a kid and in a sauerkraut factory as a teenager. None of the rest of us knew anything about cabbages. Proudly, my daughter picked the fruit—or rather vegetable—of her labor. Its final weight was 11.6 pounds, and it was as big as a bowling ball.

My daughter is hardly ever enthusiastic about vegetables, so I hoped having planted the cabbage and tended it all summer would make her more interested than usual in eating it. She looked forward to cutting it up and grating some of it in the food processor for coleslaw, and she did enjoy the first kraut burger she tried. But the honeymoon was short. Oh well, we moms can't win them all.

I have an aunt who makes the best kraut burgers on the planet, so I went straight to her for the family recipe. In other parts of the country, the dough pockets filled with ground beef, cabbage, and onion are called cabbage burgers, German burgers, Runza®, or bierocks. "Kraut" was actually a derogatory word for a German that came into use in the United States after World War I, although it doesn't generally carry the same meaning a hundred years later. So when I asked my aunt about kraut burgers, she knew I intended no offense against Germans.

Kraut burgers are easy to make. Brown a pound of ground beef with half a coarsely chopped onion. When the beef is done, drain it and add enough chopped cabbage to roughly equal the amount of hamburger in the skillet. For a pound, that's a couple of wedges of raw chopped cabbage, or about what it takes to fill an average-sized cutting board. The cabbage should be cut as thin as a dime, in small pieces, not chunks. Add a bit of garlic salt, if you like. Cook the cabbage down till it's limp in the pan, mixing well with the hamburger. Set the skillet off the heat. At this point, if you cook more than a pound of meat, the beef and cabbage can be frozen in meal-sized portions for later use.

For a simple shortcut, get a can of eight Pilsbury Grand® refrigerator biscuits. A pound of meat and a couple of wedges of cabbage will fill eight Grand biscuits, the kind in the jumbo can. On a greased cookie sheet or cake pan, flatten each biscuit with your hands to make a three- or four-inch circle. Turn the biscuit as you flatten it so the dough is even all the way across, without thin spots that will burn or allow the meat juices to seep through during baking. Place a few tablespoons of the hot beef and cabbage on the dough. Fold the dough over into a half circle. Seal the edges. Bake till the biscuit dough is golden brown, eight to ten minutes. Serve right away. To reheat in the microwave, wrap the rolls in wet paper towels so they don't dry out.

My eight-year-old daughter came across a picture of a Nativity scene behind one of the flaps in her cardboard Advent calendar as she counted down the days till Christmas. The familiar picture showed Joseph and Mary, smiling in a humble shelter, gazing at a tiny baby asleep in a manger.

"Mom," Sarah asked as she took the chocolate from the molded plastic tray in the calendar, "Jesus was born in the stable because there was no room for his parents in the inn, right?"

"That's how the story goes."

"So Mary and Joseph were poor."

"Right."

"That picture doesn't look right then. Mary and Joseph and Baby Jesus are wearing nice warm clothes, not raggedy ones. And Mary's hair would be all messy with pieces of hay in it if she'd just had a baby on the floor of the stable. She'd look really tired, with dark circles under her eyes."

Out of the mouths of babes.

Andy sidled up to my ten-year-old daughter in our back yard one hot Sunday afternoon in July, leaned shamelessly against her legs, and stole her heart before she ever knew what happened. He was scrawny, hungry, road-weary, and in dire need of a bath, but he was mannerly and affectionate nonetheless.

"Mom!" Sarah yelled through the kitchen window, knowing I'd be a soft heart for a hard case just like she was. "Come here. You need to meet somebody."

I hurried outside, wondering who my little girl was talking to. I hoped someone hadn't gotten into the yard from the alley. We always keep the gate locked, but my kid has never met a stranger in her life.

"He's so cute." Sarah put my hand on the gray and white tabby. He trembled slightly but stood his ground as I lightly petted him.

"Oh honey, not another cat," I groaned. "We've taken in one already, and this one is filthy and shedding."

"But he's not a stray." Sarah showed me the collar and matching body harness. "He's got tags. There's a phone number and a microchip ID, and the little round tag says his name is Andy."

It's too bad human beings and kitty cats haven't learned to speak the same language. Unraveling Andy's far-ranging journey turned out to be fascinating, albeit a little frustrating. I only wish the tabby cat could talk. The missing details of his epic road trip would make a best-selling book.

"Can we keep him?" Sarah asked eagerly while Andy nuzzled her hand. "See, he likes me."

"I'm sure somebody's missing him," I told her. "He's been well taken care of, and there's ID on his collar. We need to find his humans."

I began with a tag from an animal shelter in Jackson, Wyoming, near the Idaho line. Yes, Andy had been there. His shots were updated. But the man I spoke to, although polite and friendly, couldn't tell me much more than that. He was actually a deputy sheriff who took phone calls for the animal shelter on weekends. I'd have to try back during the week when the regular shelter staff were on duty, or better yet, find a no-kill sanctuary in my local area and go from there. Most places could read microchips, the deputy said. Andy would have been fitted with one before he left Jackson if he hadn't arrived with one. All dogs and cats got microchips; that was standard procedure in most U.S. facilities. Take care if you drop him off, though, the deputy warned. Reading chips was one thing, but many shelters in big cities were quick with their death needles. I promised I wouldn't be dropping Andy off anywhere till I found his home.

Next, I called the phone number on the microchip tag, which also hung from Andy's collar. I was told Andy's human had last lived in Berthoud, Colorado. I left the man a voice mail and a Facebook message.

"Berthoud is pretty far north of here," I murmured, scratching Andy behind the ears as he stretched and purred, obviously used to attention. "You sure get around, cat. What made you pick our privacy fence to shimmy under, hmmm? I guess you knew we'd keep you warm and fed while we find your people."

It took several days, but Andy's human eventually got back to me. He was worried about his cat and glad Andy had been safely found. Their reunion would be tricky to pull off, though. Andy's human had lived in Berthoud, then in Brighton, where the cat landed in my back yard. But he had recently moved to Arkansas for a new job. We thought about sending Andy with a trucker as far as Bentonville, but Sarah went ballistic.

"No way!" she screeched. "You can't do that! Ever heard of stranger danger?"

Needless to say, my little girl had fallen hard for the kitty who picked her to rescue him. She made him a comfy bed from doll blankets in her room, complete with colorful toys and a sprinkling of catnip. Andy got a bath, a brushing, and a nail trim. He and Sam-I-Am, the kitty we had taken in seven years earlier when he was young and needed a home, forged an uneasy truce after much hissing and posturing. My other half unabashedly began holding Andy like a baby several times a day and kissing him on the head. He seems to have a connection with cats that he doesn't always have with people. As for me, nobody but Almighty God heard me praying out loud that the man in Arkansas would decide it might be easier to get another cat out there and let Andy stay with my daughter ... so I'm pleading the Fifth. My lips are sealed.

I know, I know. Letting go is a valuable life lesson. Sometimes you have to say good-bye and move on. And we would, tearfully and gracefully, if and when the time came. But Andy is the friendliest cat I've ever met. He slid seamlessly into our family. I couldn't help but wonder at the time if it was meant to be. In any case, whether for the short term or the long haul, Andy chose his rescuers well.

And it seems he chose us permanently. After nearly a year, we've heard nothing more from Arkansas. I bought Andy a fish-shaped collar tag with his name engraved on one side and our phone numbers on the other, in case he ever gets lost again. He has found his new forever home.

Sleep is eluding me tonight. After gunning down thirteen innocent young people twenty years ago at Columbine High School in Colorado, two teenage boys with their whole lives ahead of them killed themselves as well, and the United States of America has never been the same.

Mass shootings have steadily become part of our cultural landscape--Newtown, San Bernardino, Las Vegas, Parkland--the list is all too familiar.

Before the terrible tragedy at Columbine, we huddled under our desks when funnel clouds drew too near, filed outside when the fire alarms blared, and groaned when spelling tests rolled around. That was pretty much as scary as school ever got, at least in the small town where I grew up.

Now even our youngest students have to deal with lock-down drills and the idea of armed assailants roaming the streets around their schools. Even if their teachers don't directly mention bad guys with guns, our children know the score. In kindergarten, my daughter Sarah faced her first lock-down drill and was afraid to return to school afterward. She wasn't worried about her own safety, since she was a Power Puff Girl®. She could handle anything the universe threw her way. Her main concern was how I would fare at home with no superhero to help me out.

As I worked at my computer last Friday afternoon, I heard the happy music of the ice cream truck on the street outside. I smiled to myself, welcoming the cheerful harbinger of spring.

Then the phone rang. It was my husband Gerald. I heard the sharp note of fear in his voice as he told me our local high school had been put on lock-down. The elementary school where our daughter attended fifth grade was on lockout, meaning no one could leave or enter the building, and all extracurricular activities would be canceled that afternoon. But the children would probably be released to their parents at the end of the day. He intended to pick our little girl up and bring her home to me in an hour or so.

My heart tightened in my chest like a clenched fist. My guts tied themselves in knots. More than anything in the world, I wanted Sarah in my arms right then. Only two days earlier, every school on the entire Front Range had been shut down because a mentally ill young woman, obsessed with the Columbine tragedy, had flown to Colorado from Miami, Florida, bought herself a shotgun and a bunch of ammunition, made credible threats about going on a shooting spree, and then disappeared. The woman had later killed herself in the mountains west of Denver, but not before closing down hundreds of schools and shaking the confidence of thousands of students, parents, teachers, and other staff members. Now here we were, held hostage once more by a situation beyond our control. The streets were full of squad cars. There were helicopters in the air. Teachers and students were trapped in the high school; parents couldn't get to their kids. I wanted my child so badly I could have moved mountains with my bare hands. All I could do was wait.

Sarah was in good spirits when her dad brought her home. Mostly she was hungry. She climbed onto my lap, asking for hugs and snacks.

"Guess what, Mom," she said. "The ice cream man was across the street from the school by the park. It's the first time I've seen him this year. I felt really bad for him. Usually we all swarm him when we first see him, but he didn't get one single customer today. Everybody ran straight to their parents. We all wanted to get right home. Because, you know, cops and everything. Poor ice cream man. I hope he isn't sad."

I hope so too. I think he might be sad, sweetheart.

Maybe the ice cream man is sitting up late, like me, wondering what can be done to protect our children. Wiser minds than mine will have to figure out what to do, I suppose. I have some ideas, but no one has asked for them, and many might fiercely disagree with them. All I know is, after twenty years, we've got to try something, because doing nothing hasn't worked. Time doesn't change anything on its own. Time, by itself, only cements the status quo in place.

Since it was a beautiful sunny day, my daughter and I went for a walk. We ended up at the playground behind her school, which is the same elementary school I attended forty years ago. On the playground is a very large, very old cottonwood tree. The school has been remodeled since I went there, so the huge old tree that used to shade the front playground is now behind the building.

Sarah decided to climb the tree, so I boosted her up, and the tenacity of her personality shone through as she schemed and struggled to get to a perch just out of her reach. She had spotted a sturdy twig, broken off and wedged between two branches, that she wanted to bring home and make a magic wand out of. I squashed the strong mom itch to tell her that climbing onto a higher limb to get the twig wasn't worth the risk, that we could find a perfectly good twig on the ground to create a wand from, that she had any number of sparkly plastic wands at home anyway--some of them even lit up. I bit back warnings about breaking bones and visiting the emergency room, but a few slipped past my lips in spite of my best efforts.

As I stood in the shade of that giant tree while Sarah finally perched safely in a fork where two parts of the trunk split off, my mind drifted back to when I was her age. I had a dear friend Belinda. She and I used to play under that same tree at recess, building "squirrel lands" and bird nests, setting up tiny dens and houses for two-bit eraser animals from the school store, picking dandelions and sticking them in lunchroom milk cartons half full of water. While the fleeting days of childhood lasted, our recess adventures in the shade of that cottonwood tree knew no bounds.

I realize childhood will pass as quickly for my daughter as it did for me. Friends who feel like sisters now will drift softly away, and eventually Sarah's mind will be weighed down with grown-up matters. But for today, it was enough for her to hear that

I was "super duper proud of her for climbing way high up in that tree."

During our long-distance flight from Denver to Detroit in the oppressive heat of August, when we attended a family wedding, my then nine-year-old daughter spent a lot of time looking out the airplane window. She enjoyed finding cats, mermaids, castles, and other formations among the clouds.

"Mom," Sarah said excitedly, "I found a whale--with feet."

"That's a new one," I answered, only half listening. "Whales don't have feet."

"This one does. It's standing at the top of a giant staircase. And there's a baby whale near it."

"Nice."

"You're not paying attention." Sarah squeezed my hand. "The whale's mouth is open wide. I see its tongue. It looks like a slide."

"Cool."

I got a few moments of silence--sweet silence. Flying isn't my thing. I mean, not at all. I hate it with red eyes of fury. I leaned back in my seat and took slow, deep breaths.

"Mom, I think I see the way into Heaven."

That grabbed me. "What? Where? Another cloud formation?"

"No, silly. You climb up the stairs to the whale's feet. Then the baby whale tells you if you get to go in or not. Whales have a language, you know. I learned that in school last year, remember? If you get to go in, you get in the big whale's mouth and slide down the tongue."

"Oh ... okay ..."

"It's beautiful inside clouds, with the sun shining in. We've flown through lots of them. I bet God and Jesus like it, kind of like stained glass windows."

I nodded. "Hmmm. True."

"Besides, Jonah got inside a whale. It's right in the Bible."

"I can't argue with that."

"I bet Jonah didn't smell very good when he got vomited out on the beach after three days, all covered with seaweed and fish spit."

"Yuck." I shuddered. "Probably not."

"So who says what the entrance to Heaven looks like, right?"

"Right. Who says?"

"I found it then."

"You might have," I agreed. "I sure can't say you didn't."

I admit, when my daughter first asked me to take her to the city park near our house so she could catch Pokemon® on my cell phone, I wasn't exactly eager to oblige her. Okay, I laughed outright.

"You want me to do what?"

"It'll be fun," Sarah coaxed. "You go to the stops and collect balls, and then you throw the balls at the Pokemon® you want and trap them. C'mon, it's a nice day."

"So Pokemon® are running all over the park like stray dogs?"

"They're everywhere. I see one in your bedroom right now. It's big, like a bull. It's swinging its three tails--swish, swish, swish! Hitting Daddy's side of the bed."

"There's a Pokemon® in my bedroom?"

"Well, just on the phone screen." My eleven-year-old patted me patiently on the shoulder, like I was hopelessly slow to catch on. "It's a brave new world."

A brave new world indeed. Phones in our pockets, computers in our hands, and strange creatures in our bedrooms. But as Sarah had said, it was a beautiful spring day. So off we went to the park.

My daughter and I have always enjoyed walks together. Ever since she was a toddler, we've collected rocks, pine cones, and flowers as we ventured along the sidewalks of the small town where we live. I worried about introducing electronics into our journeys. Would we still have fun? Would Sarah get so enamored with the phone that I became the third wheel?

I needn't have worried. Sarah found treasures in new forms at the park. She darted from place to place, as enthusiastic as she'd ever been during her toddler years, describing the Pokemon® she saw on the phone screen to me and scooping them up like precious Easter eggs from the grass. I found myself laughing with her, the same way I had when she discovered birds' nests or bunnies on other outings.

It's easy to automatically look at new ideas and innovations with suspicion. They're different. They're not comfortable or familiar, not what we grew up with. But thinking outside the box can sometimes yield wonderful surprises. Our trip to the park wasn't what we were used to, and we try to limit screen time as much as any family does, but chasing Pokemon® in the grass was a fun way to spend a gorgeous afternoon on the last day of Spring Break.

When my daughter finished her first full year of preschool at age four, it was time to celebrate. I let her decide between a trip to a nearby park and homemade ice cream sundaes, but I breathed an inward sigh of relief when she chose the sundaes. It was one of those ridiculously hot afternoons in late May when spring plays hooky and lets summer take over.

First came ice cream, then chocolate sauce. Just a dab of sauce for me, a little more for Sarah. Why not—we were celebrating, right? Then whipped cream in a can. Sarah giggled when the spray cream made its usual silly noise as it billowed magically onto her sundae.

"How do they squeeze the cream into that can?" she asked.

"I have no idea," I answered, thinking to myself that I really didn't want to know. I reached up into the cupboard for the rainbow sprinkles.

Sarah, who had been sitting on the kitchen counter watching me build the sundaes, stretched past me and grabbed a plastic jar. "I want this kind."

Thinking she had recognized her beloved rainbow sprinkles on the shelf, I didn't take time to check the bottle she gave me. I just unscrewed the cap and shook the jar generously over her sundae. I took a hard pass on the sprinkles, so I secured the lid and put the jar back in the cupboard while I made sure my daughter got down from the counter safely. She busied herself rifling through the silverware drawer for her favorite spoons with Snoopy® heads on the handles, all the while belting out the "Teamwork" song from the Wonder Pets® program that was starting on the TV in the living room.

I carried our sundaes carefully to the plastic mat we had spread on the carpet in front of the TV—and that was when the calamity happened.

I bit into my ice cream, relishing the cold, delicious bliss, and expecting a sigh of contentment from my daughter as she tasted her perfectly decadent sundae.

"Mommy!" Sarah wailed. "It's yucky! It tastes like … sh— " She gagged, then started sobbing.

"Sarah! What's wrong?"

"It tastes like …" Another gag. "Sugar!"

In preschool, Sarah had learned more than how to count to ten and distinguish her colors, which had resulted in a few serious discussions and word substitutions at our house, and I knew my distraught little girl wasn't talking about the sweet white crystals I stirred into my coffee every morning.

"Oh … don't cry … let me see." I took the sundae from her, and after one sniff, I knew. "Sarah, I put garlic on your ice cream!"

"Garlic is awful!" my daughter sniffled. "You ruined my sundae!"

My heart sank. I had wanted to make a perfect celebration sundae for Sarah. A sighted mom would never have mistaken minced garlic for rainbow sprinkles. For that matter, I would never have mistaken minced garlic for rainbow sprinkles if I had taken an extra second to feel the shape of the bottle and sniff its contents. But I'd been so sure Sarah would recognize her sprinkles and hand them to me, I'd cut corners, and now I'd ruined her sundae, ruined her celebration, ruined everything. She didn't deserve this.

"Mom?" Sarah said in a small voice as she took my hand. "You look sad. We can get more ice cream."

"Sure we can." I smiled, jolted out of my pity party. This was an easy fix. I set my dish of melting ice cream on the TV stand where my guide dog couldn't get it and carried Sarah's garlic sundae back to the kitchen. We rinsed the evidence of our goof-up down the sink, built a new sundae, complete with a generous helping of rainbow sprinkles, and settled down to watch the Wonder Pets® save the day with teamwork.

Even now, more than seven years later, we laugh about garlic sundaes when the topics of miscommunication or cooking disasters come up. Because guess what? Mistakes aren't the end of the world—not just for moms whose eyes don't work, but for everybody. Mistakes are nothing more than glitches to be gotten through and gotten over. My daughter and I both learned a lot from that garlic sundae—about grace and teamwork, about bouncing back and remembering what really matters, and about how chocolate ice cream and rainbow sprinkles can make any situation a little better.

THE END

Made in the USA
Middletown, DE
13 November 2022

14866286R00061